Peer Listening
in the Middle School:
Training Activities for Students

Sandy P.,
Best wishes
to a special
lady.
Sandy Payon

by
Sandra Peyser Hazouri
and
Miriam Frey Smith

Library of Congress
Catalog Card No. 91-075586

ISBN 0-932796-34-6

Publisher—
Educational Media Corporation®
PO Box 21311
Minneapolis, MN 55421
(612) 781-0088

Production editor—
Don L. Sorenson

Graphic design—
Earl Sorenson

Illustrator—
Christine M. Brown

Sandra Peyser Hazouri and Miriam Frey Smith

Dedication

This book is dedicated to our children:

David Hazouri

Sharon Hazouri

Becky Smith

Sarah Smith

Lauren Smith

whose middle school experiences have been
a continuing inspiration.

About the Authors

Sandra Peyser Hazouri is a school counseling consultant for the State Department of Public Instruction in Raleigh, North Carolina. She has served as a teacher, counselor, and peer program supervisor. She has contributed to the field of peer work by doing state and national training workshops and by serving as the President of the North Carolina Peer Helper Association. Ms. Hazouri is a native of Miami, Florida and resides in Raleigh, North Carolina with her children.

Miriam Frey Smith is the prevention training consultant for the State Department of Public Instruction in Raleigh, North Carolina. She is a state and national trainer for peer programming and a member of the Board of the North Carolina Peer Helper Association. Ms. Smith is the author of numerous educational articles and co-author of the nationally acclaimed parent training manual, *D.A.R.E. to Parent.* Ms. Smith is a native of Massachusetts. She currently resides in Raleigh, North Carolina.

Table of Contents

Sandra Peyser Hazouri and Miriam Frey Smith

Welcome, Peer Listener:

This is *your* workbook. It is intended to guide you through a new kind of learning experience. You will be practicing skills that you will learn in this book to help you perform services to your fellow students. These skills will enhance your own life as well.

You will have opportunities to use your special talents and to discover your unique gifts. You will learn to reach out to others and to know yourself better. You will grow as a person and others will grow because of you.

To be successful, you will have to take some risks, learn to trust others, and have faith in yourself. This book is designed to help you accomplish all these things and more. Get ready for a great adventure. Good luck!

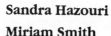

Sandra Hazouri
Miriam Smith

Programs and Projects
for Peer Listeners

Here are some programs and projects in which you can effectively participate after you have completed the training activities in this book.

Activity Leaders

Peer Listeners can go into advisement and homebased programs and teach the activities in this book to others.

Cross Age Tutoring

Peer Listeners can assist younger students in the school with academics and skill building.

Co-Leaders for Small Discussion Groups

Peer Listeners can work with guidance counselors to lead small group discussions on relevant adolescent topics.

Sponsors and Promoters of School-Wide Events

Peer Listening Classes can serve as sponsors of poster contests, spirit weeks, Wall of Fame (recognition bulletin board), and so forth.

Community Service Projects

Peer Listeners can serve the community through senior citizen visitation, collecting food for the needy, and other community based activities.

Lunch Buddies

Peer Listeners can be assigned to students that have just moved to the area and do not know anyone in the middle school. A Peer Listener is assigned to eat lunch with a new student for two weeks, to introduce the new student to other students, and to answer questions that come up each day.

Big Brothers/Big Sisters and Orientation to the Middle School

Peer Listeners can talk to fifth or sixth grade students who are about to enter the middle school, addressing their fears and correcting any misinformation these students may have about the middle school.

Homework Buddies/Absentee Buddies

Peer Listeners can insure that absent students get homework assignments. Peer Listeners can call absent students to let them know that they were missed.

Peer Pen Pals

Peer Listeners can write to elementary school classes during the year, sharing their middle school experiences.

Listening to Others

Peer Listeners can listen to others, using the skills they have learned in this book. They can keep a log of listening activities to share with their peer leader.

Chapter I
Introduction to
Peer Listening

Be sure to look for...

☐ **Peer Listener Pledge**

☐ **Qualities of a Listener**

☐ **Storytelling**

- Do you remember a time when you had something on your mind and everyone around you seemed too busy to listen?

- Are there some things going on in your life that only someone your age would understand?

- Have you ever felt embarrassed by the idea of talking to an adult about your problems?

- When something great happens, do you look around for someone to tell?

You have had some of these experiences and so have most other middle school students. In fact, most of the problems people have are everyday problems. These are the things that cause us a small amount of discomfort. These problems may make us feel mad, embarrassed, excited, worried, or even scared, but they are not serious enough to take to a counselor. People don't usually need help with everyday problems, but they need someone to listen to them. Middle School Peer Listeners fill the bill!

In middle school you are at a point in your life when you're experiencing many changes. You are beginning to mature; you are making some big decisions; and you are making new friends. You are beginning to explore and try new things. Perhaps some of these concerns are familiar to you.

"Am I wearing the right clothes?"

"Are my parents too strict?"

"Am I too short to try out for basketball?"

"Should I join the PEP club?"

These are just a few of the everyday problems of middle school students. These students need someone to "bounce" things off of. They need someone who will take the time to listen, to understand their feelings—someone who will not laugh at them or put them down.

Sometimes students have more serious problems that they want to talk about. For example;

"I broke up with my boyfriend."

"I'm failing math."

"My best friend moved away."

"My girlfriend wants me to try a beer."

These students may just need someone to listen. Sometimes they need to go to an adult for help.

Once in a while a friend may come to you with a very serious problem. For example:

"My uncle touches me all the time and wants me to touch him."

"I'm very sad. Life isn't worth living."

As a Peer Listener, you will be taught how to refer these students to an adult so they can get the help they need.

What does it take to be a Peer Listener? You have brought some of the qualities of a good listener with you to this program. You may be very interested in people, very understanding of others, or you may be a person who is easy to be with. These qualities will be strengthened and others will be developed as you work with your class to better understand yourself and others. Along with these important qualities, you need some special skills to become a successful Peer Listener. The training you will receive through your Peer Listening Class will help you to handle your new responsibilities well. Skills and qualities combine to help you grow as a person and to be a better friend to others.

Activity 1

Rules and Regs

Purpose:

To define the rules of the Peer Listening Group for working together.

Materials:

Newsprint, magic markers

Procedure:

1. With the class, brainstorm a list of everything you can think of that is important for a group to do to work well together. Your leader may have some rules to add that are not open for discussion or change. These include meeting times and class membership which are often decided prior to the beginning of the class. However, these should be part of the list. Be sure to write all of the suggestions on the board.

2. As a class, discuss those rules that are important to a Peer Listening Class and will keep it running smoothly.

3. Vote as a class on each rule and choose the four or five that receive the highest votes.

4. Add the Peer Listener Pledge to the list.

5. Ask for volunteers to make the list into a permanent poster and bring it to the next class.

6. Ask for a volunteer to write the Peer Listener Pledge on the board or on newsprint.

7. With your class, stand and recite the Peer Listener Pledge.

8. Applaud yourselves.

Peer Listener Pledge

I pledge to keep confidential the information that friends and other students share with me. If I am concerned about a student harming himself, herself, or others, I will tell a responsible adult or peer leader immediately. I will also inform the student of my decision.

Activity 2

Pretest: Peer Listening Inventory

Purpose:

To assess your Peer Listening Skills before training begins.

Materials:

Peer Listening Inventory, pencil

Procedure:

1. Your leader will introduce the concept of a pretest and make sure everyone understands its purpose. The pretest is to be checked but not graded.

2. Take the *Peer Listening Inventory.* Collect the sheets and put them in a folder to be saved until the end of the training.

3. You will take the *Peer Listening Inventory* again at the end of the training.

Peer Listening Inventory

T F   1. All problems should be discussed with an adult.

T F   2. Most problems are very serious.

T F   3. Building trust is an important part of Peer Listening.

T F   4. Put downs are a form of compliment.

T F   5 Every person is important.

T F   6. Every person is unique.

T F   7. All human beings have needs.

T F   8. Capable means able to do.

T F   9. Listening is done only with your ears.

T F 10. You can communicate anger with your eyes.

T F 11. Saying "You must be happy" to an excited person is clarifying that person's feelings.

T F 12. Recognizing your own feelings has nothing to do with the feelings of others.

T F 13. There is one best way to respond to a person with a problem.

T F 14. A good way to respond to someone is to check for feelings.

T F 15. Peer Listeners should put another person's problems ahead of everything in their own lives.

T F 16. You should keep all problems confidential.

T F 17. Consequences are positive and negative outcomes.

T F 18. A Peer Listener should choose an alternative for a friend.

T F 19. Making a decision is easy.

T F 20. When you finish this book, you will need no follow-up training.

Activity 3
Who is Listening?

Purpose:

To identify the qualities of a good listener.

Materials:

Paper, magic markers, large newsprint

Procedure:

1. On a piece of paper, list the people that you have gone to when you felt embarrassed, afraid, upset, or excited— people that have been good listeners in your life.

2. In small groups, make a list on newsprint of the kinds of people that the group members consider to be good listeners in their lives. List these people on the left side of the newsprint.

3. Discuss as a group the qualities these people have that make them good listeners.

4. List these qualities on the right side of the newsprint.

5. Share the group list with the class.

6. Post the lists on the wall and circle the qualities that showed up on the lists most often.

7. Take a class vote on the one most important quality of a Peer Listener.

Activity 4

The Meaning of the Words

Purpose:

To define the qualities of a Peer Listener.

Materials:

Newsprint or poster board, magic markers

Procedure:

1. Divide the class into small groups.

2. Divide the list of qualities of a Peer Listener that you obtained from Activity 3 among the small groups. Each group should have at least one quality to define and it should be different from the others.

3. With your group, come up with a definition of the quality. For example, if your group has the word "caring," you will decide as a group what caring means.

4. With your group, think of an example of the quality. For example, you would say, "A caring person is someone who...."

5. Write your word in large letters on newsprint. Write your group's definition and example underneath.

6. Put your newsprint on the wall and share your group's definition and example with the rest of the class.

7. Applaud the efforts.

8. Leave the newsprint posted, or make a smaller poster with the qualities listed, as a reminder at each class meeting.

Activity 5

Storytelling

Purpose:

To identify the characteristics and feelings of someone who needs a listener.

Materials:

Paper and pencil

Procedure:

1. Think of a time when you or someone you know needed someone to talk to about a concern.

2. Write a short story about this time, beginning your story with "Once upon a time" and changing the names of all the people involved.

3. Include the following information in your story:

   a. What happened? Why did the person in your story need someone to talk with?

   b. What was the person in your story thinking and feeling?

   c. Did the person find someone to listen?

   d. Did the person's feelings change after talking to someone? How?

   e. If the person in your story did not find a listener, how did that person feel?

4. Ask for volunteers to share their stories with the class.

5. With your class, list on the left side of the board the thoughts and feelings the people in the stories were having when they needed someone to listen.

6. On the right side of the board, make a list of thoughts and feelings the people in the stories had when someone listened to them.

Activity 6

Practice Practice

Purpose:

To practice the ideas that you learned in this chapter outside the classroom.

Materials:

None

Procedure:

1. Find three people in your school who need someone to listen to them, and listen to their concerns. Remember to demonstrate some of the qualities of a good Peer Listener that you identified in Activity 3 and defined in Activity 4.

2. When you return to your Peer Listening Class, discuss the following questions:

    a. How did you identify the people who needed someone to listen? (Do not use real names.) How did they look? What did they say?

    b. What were the problems they talked about? (Remember, do not use real names.)

    c. Did you know what to do or say?

    d. What difficulties did you have?

Activity 7
Looking at My Skills

Purpose:

To summarize and evaluate the concepts that you learned in this chapter.

Materials:

None

Procedure:

1. On this page, write how you feel about your skill level as a beginning Peer Listener.

2. Include some reflection on your practice experience.

   a. What happened that makes you proud?

   b. What would you do differently next time?

   c. In what area do you need improvement?

My Reflections:

_____

_____

_____

_____

_____

_____

_____

_____

_____

Sandra Peyser Hazouri and Miriam Frey Smith

Chapter II
Getting to Know
Each Other

Be sure to look for...

❏ **Blindfold Your Partner**

❏ **Lining Up by Birthdays**

❏ **Becoming a Toaster**

Learning the skills to become a Peer Listener requires teamwork. Teamwork means working with a group towards a common goal. To be successful, members of the team must be able to recognize how they are different. The team will want to use the special skills and abilities of each individual.

People have characteristics that are common to everyone. All people have physical similarities like ears, noses, and fingernails. All people also have needs, feelings, beliefs, thoughts, and abilities. The individual differences in physical appearance and in thoughts, needs, feelings, beliefs, and abilities are what make each person special and unique.

As you begin to accept and appreciate your team members, you will begin to gain each other's trust. You will come to know that your personal sharing will be kept confidential. You will take your team members' problems seriously and they will treat your problems as important. They will not laugh at you and you will not put them down. This is the beginning of friendship, an important asset for a Peer Listener.

Activity 8
The Interview: Alike Under the Skin

Purpose:

To discover how much we have in common with each other.

Materials:

Pencil, paper

Procedure:

1. Write the month you were born in big letters on a piece of paper and hold it up.

2. Pair up with someone who was born the same month as you. (If there is no one, look for the month before or the month after yours.)

3. Ask each other the interview questions that follow.

4. Find some things you have in common.

5. Introduce your partner to the class and share with the class two things you and your partner have in common.

Interview Questions:

1. What kind of music do you listen to most often?
   _____

2. Do you have any brothers or sisters?_____
   Are they older or younger? _____

3. Do you play a sport?_____
   What is it?_____

4. Where were you born?_____

5. What do you do for fun?_____

6. What do you like *best* about school?_____
   What do you like *least* about school?_____

7. What reasons do you have for becoming a Peer Listener?
   _____

Activity 9

The Trust Experience

Purpose:

To experience the feelings of being trusted and of trusting others.

Materials:

Blindfolds

Procedure:

1. Find a partner. This exercise works best with someone who is not a close friend.

2. Decide with your partner who will be partner A and who will be partner B. Blindfold partner A.

3. Partner B carefully *guides* partner A around the room using voice commands. It is acceptable to hold partner A's hand or to do anything else that makes partner A feel secure. However, partner B cannot *lead* partner A around the room. You are responsible for your partner's safety.

4. After three minutes, change roles with your partner. At this time partner B will be blindfolded and partner A will give the voice commands to guide partner B around the room. (This exercise may be done outside.)

5. Following this exercise, discuss these questions as a class:

   a. How did it feel to know that your blindfolded partner was trusting you to guide you safely?

   b. Did anything happen while you were blindfolded that made you doubt that your partner was trustworthy? If so, were you able to regain your trust? How?

   c. What feelings do you have toward someone you trust?

   d. Why do Peer Listeners need to trust each other?

Activity 10
Birthday Bunches

Purpose:

To establish small work groups within the larger class.

Materials:

None

Procedure:

1. Designate the left wall of the room January 1st. Designate the right wall of the room December 31st.

2. *Without talking*, line up across the room according to your birth date. For example, if your birthday is in January, you would be very close to the left wall of the room. If your birthday is in June, you would be in the middle.

3. After a straight line is formed, call out your birth date beginning with the student closest to the left wall.

4. Beginning again at the end of the line, count off in fours or sixes, depending on the size of your class. The first four or six people will form a small group, the second four or six people will form another small group and so on. Small groups should plan to sit together for the Peer Listener Training Sessions to follow.

Activity 11
Making It Work

Purpose:

To begin working together in small groups.

Materials:

Paper

Procedure:

1. Write the name of machines listed below (or make up your own) on small slips of paper and distribute one slip of paper to each small group. Keep your machine assignments a secret.

fire engine	tow truck
popcorn machine	television
typewriter	video game
toaster	copy machine
gas pump	

2. As a group, decide how to build the machine using only the bodies of all of your group members. You will want to do it in a way that other groups can guess what kind of machine you have built.

3. Practice building your machine. For example, if your group had the assignment of a washing machine, you might hold hands to form a circle, while one student in the middle twists back and forth like the agitator in a washing machine.

4. Build your machine for the other groups, and allow them to guess your machine. Be sure that all efforts get applause!

5. In your small group, discuss what grade you would give yourselves for working together by answering the following questions:

   a. Did everyone cooperate?

   b. Were there any put downs?

   c Were everyone's ideas listened to?

   d. Did everyone have a vote in the discussion?

6. Share with the class why your group thinks it is important for Peer Listeners to learn to cooperate.

Activity 12

Let's Take a Commercial Break

Purpose:

To learn about working together as a team.

Materials:

None

Procedure:

1. List, as a group, some of the qualities you like about your small group. For example, you may all bring different talents to the group or you may all be very caring people.

2. Discuss, as a group, ways that you could advertise these qualities to the class. You may want to think about the different kinds of advertisements and commercials you see on television.

3. Make up a commercial about your group. Remember, commercials are short, attention getting, and make just one or two points. Some suggestions:
   - a jingle or rhyme
   - a rap
   - an interview
   - an imitation of a well known commercial.

4. Perform your commercial for the class. Be sure to applaud all efforts.

5. Grade your small group on how well you worked together by answering the following questions:
   a. Did everyone participate?
   b. Were everyone's ideas listened to?
   c. Were there any put downs?
   d. Did everyone have a vote in the decisions?

6. Share why you think it is important for Peer Listeners to work together.

Activity 13
Practice Practice

Purpose:

To practice the skills that you learned in this chapter outside the classroom.

Materials:

None

Procedure:

1. Find someone at school you do not know. Get acquainted and learn about three things that you have in common.

2. When you return to your Peer Listening Class, discuss the following questions:

   a. Who did you meet? (Names are okay here.)

   b. How did you meet this person?

   c. What three things do you have in common with this person?

   d. What was difficult about this activity?

Activity 14
Looking at My Skills

Purpose:

To summarize and evaluate the that you skills learned in this chapter.

Materials:

None

Procedure:

1. On this page, write how you feel about your skill level in getting to know others.

2. Include some reflection on your practice experience.

   a. Is it difficult or not for you to meet a stranger? Why is this so?

   b. What happened that made you proud?

   c. What would you do differently next time?

   d. In what area do you need improvement?

My Reflections:

_____

_____

_____

_____

_____

_____

_____

_____

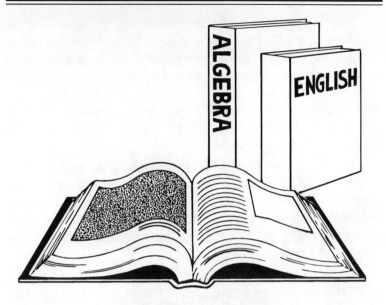

Chapter III
Getting to Know Yourself

Be sure to look for...

❑ **Red Hair Like Grandma**

❑ **Correcting Your Data**

❑ **Messages On Your Back**

Knowing yourself and liking who you are has to happen before you can know and like other people. Individual differences in people are what make them interesting and special. Your acceptance of your own individual differences helps you to appreciate the specialness of others.

Your strengths and weakness's are part of that difference. You may be good at cooking and have a friend who is good at using the computer. These are strengths and they are easy to accept. It is often harder to accept weaknesses. Human beings tend to focus on their weaknesses and make them larger and more important than they really are. It is important to remember that your weaknesses are a very small part of what makes you a whole and special person.

Some of these strengths and weaknesses, as well as some personality characteristics, talents, and your physical appearance, are inherited through your biological parents. Values, beliefs, and ideas about yourself and the world come, in part, from the family you belong to and the community or neighborhood where you are growing up.

You are a special combination of all of these things and many more characteristics that are uniquely your own. Feeling good about yourself has to do with accepting this special combination that makes you the person you are.

Your brain is like a computer. It takes all the information you feed into it and stores it. Your self-esteem—how you feel about yourself—is the result of information from other people (family, friends, teachers, and so forth) and from yourself that you have stored in your brain's computer. If most of the information you have stored about yourself is positive, your self-esteem is probably pretty high. If you have a lot of negative information about yourself stored in your brain's computer, your self-esteem is most likely low.

You can erase and change information on a computer. Your brain is no different. You can erase or take out information that does not help you to feel good about yourself. You can also choose what information you feed into your brain's computer.

You are in control of your self-esteem. In fact you can choose to know and love yourself.

Activity 15
Going My Way

Purpose:

To explore your own unique way of thinking and feeling.

Materials:

Newsprint, magic markers, index cards, and tape

Procedure:

1. At the top of individual sheets of newsprint, print the following titles: SHOES, DINNER, WEATHER, ANIMAL, BUILDING, DESSERT.

2. Tape the sheets of newsprint on the walls around the room.

3. Each student should receive six index cards.

4. On your index cards, write one thing within each category that best describes you in big letters.

5. On the back of the index card, explain your choice in one or two sentences. For example:

   • TRANSPORTATION—pickup truck; I'm from the country and that's what we drive.

   • DESSERT—apple pie; I'm plain on the outside and warm and sweet on the inside.

   You do not have to share your reasons with anyone unless you choose to.

6. Tape your index cards under the appropriate categories on the wall.

7. Volunteers share with the class their reasons why they are like a certain kind of shoe, dessert, and so forth. Applaud volunteers who are willing to share.

8. Discuss with your class how many differences there are under each category.

9. Discuss why there is no right or wrong response in this exercise.

Activity 16

It's Me

Purpose:

To explore what is important to you.

Materials:

Construction paper, crayons or magic markers, magazines, and a picture of you from home, if available

Procedure:

1. Glue your picture to the top of the construction paper, or draw a picture of yourself. Write your full name under the picture. If you have a nickname, write it under your full name.

2. Using words, drawings, magazine pictures, or all three, decorate the paper with the answers to the following statements;

   a. I am happiest when _____

   b. I need _____

   c. I wish _____

   d. I am proudest of _____

   e. I love _____

   f. I am usually _____

   g. My favorite possession is _____

   h. What I want most is _____

3. Share your picture with your class. Explain any pictures you may have used.

4. Walk around the class sharing others' pictures.

5. Take your picture home to hang in your room.

Activity 17

Your Genetic Secrets

Purpose:

To learn more about yourself by surveying your family.

Materials:

Questionnaire, pencil

Procedure:

1. Take your book or a copy of the questionnaire home.

2. Show your family members the questions and ask for their help in answering them. It is important to survey grandparents, aunts, uncles, and older cousins, as well as your parents.

3. In a small group, share something you learned about yourself from looking at and talking to your family.

4. In your small group, list ways this activity was helpful to you. For example, you may have learned that most of your family members are short and that you will probably be short also.

Questionnaire

How tall were your mother and father when they were your age? Mother: _____ Father: _____

How tall are they now? Mother: _____ Father: _____

Do you have any grandparents, aunts, or uncles who are unusually tall or unusually short? _____

How tall or short? _____

Did your mother and father always have the color hair they have now? Mother: _____ Father: _____ If not, what color was it? _____

How old were your mother and father when they began to show signs of maturing? (reaching puberty) Mother: _____ Father: _____

Are there others in your family that have special gifts or talents like yours? (works well with one's hands, good at sports, musical, artistic, good reader, good sense of humor)? _____ Who are the persons and what are the gifts? _____

Person	Gift
_____	_____
_____	_____
_____	_____

What have family members done for work or careers?

Great grandfathers/mothers _____

Grandfathers/ mothers _____

Aunts/uncles _____

Parents _____

Are any of the careers alike or similar? _____

How or why did they choose these careers? _____
_____

What are some characteristics that many of your family members have in common? (freckles, a certain shaped nose, small or big feet, hair color) _____

Does your family ever tell you that you resemble another family member? _____ What is the resemblance? _____ Do you agree? _____

Activity 18

Feed Your Own Computer

Purpose:

To understand how you can control your beliefs about yourself.

Materials:

Practice Data Sheet, pencil

Procedure:

1. Working on your own, read the *Practice Data Sheet*.

2. Think of each statement as incorrect data that needs correcting before it can become part of your complete program.

3. Write the corrected version of the data on the blank lines beside the incorrect data. Notice that most incorrect data are general statements based on a single incident.

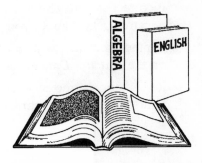

Practice Data Sheet

For example

Incorrect Data   **Corrected Data**

| You missed the basket. | I missed one basket. |

| You are a terrible basketball player. | I usually play pretty well. |

Someone says to you or you say to yourself:

Incorrect Data   **Corrected Data**

| I have a pimple; I am so ugly | |

| You haven't finished the dishes. What a lazy person! | |

| You got a bad grade on that test. STUPID! | |

4. Now work on your personal data sheet. On the left, list some incorrect data that is presently stored in your computer. Incorrect data may be criticisms or put downs from others or negative beliefs about yourself.

5. On the right side, write a corrected version just as you did on the *Practice Data Sheet*.

6. Reread the corrected data you have just written. Picture yourself feeding the corrected data into your brain's computer.

From: Hazouri, S. P.; & Smith, M.F. (1991). Peer listening in the Middle School. Minn: Educational Media Corp

Miriam Frey Smith

7. Discuss with your class how easy or difficult it was to correct your data.

8. Discuss with your class how you can correct future negative data before it becomes part of your computer program.

Personal Data Sheet

Incorrect Data   **Correct Data**

Activity 19
Messages for Me

Purpose:

To identify some of the positive characteristics others see in you.

Materials:

Plain white legal sized paper, tape, and water soluble thin magic markers

Procedure:

1. Tape a piece of plain white paper to your back.

2. Using a water soluble thin marking pen, write short, positive messages on the backs of other students and ask them to write messages on your back. The message should say something specific about the other person. For example: "You ask great questions" or "I like your red hair." Write messages to as many students as possible in the time allowed.

3. Read your messages

4. With your class, discuss how it feels to read positive things about yourself.

5. Talk about why people don't send more positive messages to each other.

Activity 20
Practice Practice

Purpose:

To practice the skills that you learned in this chapter outside the class.

Materials:

None

Procedure:

1. Ask each family member to identify two positive characteristics they see in you or two things they like about you.

2. When you return to your Peer Listening Class, discuss the following questions:

   a. What were some of the things your family said about you?

   b. Did anything they said surprise you?

   c. Did more than one family member say the same thing?

   d. Was it difficult for you to hear positive things about yourself?

Activity 21
Looking at My Skills

Purpose:

To summarize and evaluate the skills that you learned in this chapter.

Materials:

None

Procedure:

1. On this page, write how you feel about yourself, including new things you have learned about yourself in this class.

2. Include some reflection on your practice experience.

   a. How did you feel when you were hearing positive comments about yourself?

   b. What did you say to the family member?

   c. How does what your family said about you fit with what you believe about yourself?

   d. What will you do from now on when you receive a compliment?

My Reflections:

_____

_____

_____

_____

_____

_____

_____

_____

Chapter IV
Understanding Our
Humanness

Be sure to look for...

❑ **The Skin Horse**

❑ **Joining a Secret Club**

❑ **Different Families**

All human beings have needs that must be met in order to live healthy, happy lives. Everyone needs water and a certain amount of food, the ability to eliminate waste and to rest, and everyone needs to have some form of shelter. These needs must be met for the human *body* to survive.

There are other needs that must be met for the human *spirit* to survive.

The need to feel secure.

You may know that babies need to feel safe and protected. What you may not realize is that all human beings have that same need to feel safe and protected throughout their lives.

The need to belong.

If you have ever moved to a different neighborhood or gone to a new school, you know the feeling of wanting to belong. All human beings have the need to feel connected to others, to fit in, and to be a member of a group.

The first group a human being becomes a member of is the family. Families come in many different forms. In some families, parents, grandparents, children, aunts, and uncles all live in the same house. Another family might consist of one parent and one child. In still another family, the person who takes care of the children may not be the parent at all.

The need to be loved.

All human beings need to feel cherished (loved and valued) by the people close to them. It is by feeling accepted and important to others that we learn to love ourselves.

The need to feel capable.

Capable means able to do. All human beings need to feel able to do what their lives require them to do. People need to feel in charge of their lives. For example, if you are in the seventh grade, you have a need to feel capable of seventh grade work. It is the feeling of being capable that allows you to try new things, make decisions, and move forward in your life. Good self-esteem—feeling okay about who you are—comes from having these basic needs met. There are many people—many students your age—who do not feel loved, accepted, safe, or capable of handling their middle school experiences. They have low self-esteem. Trained Peer Listeners can make a difference to these students.

Activity 22

The People Picture

Purpose:

To explore human needs as a way of understanding yourself and others.

Materials:

Large piece of newsprint, magic markers

Procedure:

1. Brainstorm as a class all of the needs of human beings.

2. In your small group, talk about the needs human beings have when they are babies and how those needs change or stay the same as people get older.

3. Have a member of your group draw four figures in a row on the newsprint. The first figure should represent a baby, the second a small child, the third a teenager, and the fourth an adult.

4. Under each figure, list the needs that person has at that age. Choose the same color marker to use when the need is the same for every age group. For example, if your group believes that people need to feel loved at every age, you might write that in purple under each figure.

5. Post the completed pictures on the wall and answer the following questions as a class from the posted pictures.

   a. What are some needs that all human beings have in common?

   b. Are there needs that are special to being a teenager? What are they?

   c. What was one thing you learned today about being a human being?

Sandra Peyser Hazouri and Miriam Frey Smith

Activity 23

My Human Needs

Purpose:

To explore how these human needs are met in your life.

Materials:

None

Procedure:

1. Complete the following statements:

   a. Some choices or decisions I have made this year that I feel good about are _____

   b. Groups I belong to are _____

   c. Places where I feel safe are _____

   d. Ways my family shows me they love me are_____
      _____

2. Share your answers with one other person.

Activity 24

How Far Will You Go to Belong?

Purpose:

Learning the difference between the need to belong and giving in to peer pressure.

Materials:

None

Procedure:

1. Discuss as a class the need that people have to belong. List on the board all the groups (religious, civic, school) that members belong to.

2. Were there any kinds of initiation required in order to belong to these groups? If yes, list them on the board.

3. Class members read the following story and answer the questions. Then share the answers in groups of three.

The Secret Club

Louise has been asked to join a secret club at school. It has no adult leaders and some secret rules (no telling parents). In order to join you must smoke five cigarettes and drink three beers. Louise doesn't know what to do. Many of the most popular kids at school belong to this club, yet she doesn't believe in smoking or drinking. "Maybe I just need to change myself to fit in with this crowd," she thinks.

1. Do you know of clubs or groups that require a test for new membership? What are the requirements?

2. Have you ever been as confused as Louise about what to do?

3. What did you do and how did you feel?

Activity 25
Family Collage

Purpose:

To look at the different kinds of families.

Materials:

Magazines, glue, construction paper

Procedure:

1. Divide into small groups. Working with your group, look for pictures that could represent a kind of family. For example, a picture of an old man and a small boy could represent a family where the child lives with the grandparents.

2. Cut out and glue pictures in a collage on construction paper.

3. Explain to the rest of the class the different kinds of families represented in your group's collage.

Activity 26
Families Care

Purpose:

To show how family members love and care about each other.

Materials:

None

Procedure:

1. Read the following situations and answer the questions as though each one happened at your house.

   a. You say you will be home right after school. You don't come home until 5:00. Who will care? _____
   Why? _____

   b. You come home from a party looking sad, but you say everything is okay. Who will care? _____
   Why? _____

   c. You go on a crash diet and don't eat anything but carrots for a week. Who will care? _____
   Why? _____

   d. You shave off half the hair on your head. Who will care?
   _____
   Why? _____

2. Write two family situations that might really happen in your home. Share with the class who will care and why.

Activity 27

Giant Steps

Purpose:

To identify how capable you believe you are.

Materials:

None

Procedure:

1. A class volunteer serves as the caller.

2. With your class, form a row at one end of a room with the caller at the other end of the room. The room should be free of furniture.

3. With your class, follow the directions of the caller. The game will end when one (or more) student reaches the opposite end of the room.

4. Practice with these examples: If you are able to write a poem, take one giant step forward (pause). If you are able to ride a bike, take one giant step and two baby steps (pause).

5. Now start the game, with everyone on the starting line.

6. At the end of the game, discuss the following questions:

   a. Why did some students finish ahead of others?

   b. What did this game show you about what you believe about yourself?

   c. Can you tell from this game which members of the class have the highest self-esteem? How can you tell?

Caller: (Read loudly)

If you are able to make a bed, take one giant step (pause).

If you are able to sing, take two baby steps (pause).

If you are able to chop wood, take one baby step (pause).

If you are able to run a mile, take two giant steps (pause).

If you believe you are not able to do math, take three baby steps and one giant step backward (pause).

If you are able to wash dishes, take one giant step and one baby step (pause).

If you are able to catch a ball, take one giant step (pause).

If you believe you are not able to cook, take one giant step backward (pause).

If you are able to draw, take one giant step and one baby step (pause).

If you are able to climb a tree, take three baby steps (pause).

If you believe you are not able to walk a mile, take one giant step backward (pause).

If you are able to operate a computer, take two giant steps (pause).

If you are able to babysit, take four baby steps (pause).

If you are able to name all fifty states, take two giant steps (pause).

If you are able to operate a washing machine, take one giant step and one baby step (pause).

If you believe you are not able to dance, take one giant step backward (pause).

If you are able to recite the words from the song, *America the Beautiful*, take two giant steps.

Activity 28
What is Real?

Purpose:

To explore the need people have to be loved and cared for.

Materials:

Paper, magic markers, and crayons

Procedure:

1. A volunteer or the leader reads *What Is Real* aloud to the class.

2. With your class, discuss the following questions:

    a. How does the Skin Horse define "real?"

    b. What does the phrase "Real is not how you are made, it's a thing that happens to you" mean?

    c. What does the story say about how a person feels when one knows one is cared for and loved?

3. Complete the stick figure picture like a middle school student who fits the story's description of "real."

4. Share your picture with the rest of the class.

What is Real?

"What is REAL?" asked the Rabbit one day when he was lying beside the Skin Horse near the nursery fender, before Nana came to tidy the room. "Does it mean having things that buzz inside you and a stick-out handle?"

"Real isn't how you are made," said the Skin Horse. "It's a thing that happens to you. When a child loves you for a long, long time, not just to play with, but REALLY loves you, then you become REAL."

"It doesn't happen all at once," said the Skin Horse. "You become. It takes a long time. That's why it doesn't often happen to people who break easily, or have sharp edges, or who have to be carefully kept. Generally, by the time you are Real, most of your hair has been loved off, and your eyes drop out, and you get loose in the joints and very shabby. But these things don't matter at all, because once you are Real you can't be ugly, except to people who don't understand."

(Adapted from *The Velveteen Rabbit* by Margery Williams)

Activity 29
Practice Practice

Purpose:

To practice the skills that you learned in this chapter outside the classroom.

Materials:

None

Procedure:

1. Find three students who do not belong to any clubs or teams at school, explain what you are doing, and ask them each for an interview.

2. Ask them the following questions:

   a. Why have you not joined any of the clubs or teams at school?

   b. Would you join a club or team if you had the opportunity?

   c. How do you spend your free time?

   d. What do you like best about _____ Middle School?

3. When you return to class, share the results with the other members. (Do not use real names.)

4. Discuss the following questions:

   a. What was the most common reason for not belonging to a club or team?

   b. Do you think these students are happier or unhappier than students who belong to clubs and teams?

   c. Were the interviews difficult? If so, why?

Activity 30
Looking at My Skills

Purpose:

To summarize and evaluate the skills that you learned in this chapter.

Materials:

None

Procedure:

1. On this page, write how you feel about your level of understanding of human beings.

2. Include some reflection on your practice experience.

    a. What did you learn about the need to belong?

    b. What happened in the interview that you feel good about?

    c. What would you do differently next time?

My Reflections:

_____

_____

_____

_____

_____

_____

_____

_____

_____

Chapter V
Listening Skills, Verbal and Non-Verbal

Be sure to look for...

❏ **Your Favorite Song**

❏ **Using Your Eyes Effectively**

❏ **Tiger Lake**

Listening

Are you wondering why a whole chapter of this book is about listening? Most people think listening is a simple skill—just an exchange of words between people. Actually there are many ways to listen.

You listen with your eyes when you look at someone who is talking. Eye contact shows that you are paying attention and are interested in what is being said. You also show interest by nodding and leaning toward the person who is speaking. Saying things like "Tell me more" or "I see" encourages the speaker to continue.

When you don't give your full attention to someone who is talking to you, the person will probably feel that you don't care about what is being said. When you are listening, avoid talking about your own problems or doing something else while the other person is talking. Good listening requires focused attention.

Questioning

A good listener also asks questions.

There are two kinds of questions that people ask each other, *open* and *closed*. *Closed* questions can usually be answered by one or two words. The answer to a closed question is often "yes" or "no." For example, "Do you like to read?" "Are you going to the dance?"

An *open* question requires a longer, more personal answer. The answer to an open question has a lot more information in it. For example, "What do you like to read?" "How do you feel about going to the dance?"

In this chapter you will be doing activities that will check to see how well you really listen. You will learn to practice attentive listening using other parts of your body besides your ears. Finally, you will learn to ask questions that encourage others to share. Isn't that what Peer Listening is all about?

Activity 31

Are You Listening?

Purpose:

To understand the need for careful listening.

Materials:

Plain white paper, pencil

Procedure:

1. Find a partner. Decide who will be partner A and who will be partner B.

2. Sit back to back with your partner.

3. Partner A will read the instructions below while partner B draws a picture according to the instructions. Partner B may not ask any questions.

   Directions:

   a. Draw a small circle in the center of the paper.

   b. Draw a line straight down from the circle.

   c. Halfway down the line make a long oval shape on the left side of the line that touches the line.

   d. Draw half circles around the small circle in the center of the paper.

4. Partner B tell Partner A what has been drawn.

5. Discuss the following questions:

   a. What was difficult about this exercise?

   b. What would have made this exercise easier?

   c. Did Partner A want to look at Partner B's drawing?

   d. Did Partner B want to ask questions?

Activity 32

The Paper Game

Purpose:

To experience listening for content.

Materials:

Strips of plain paper 2" x 7"

Procedure:

1. Each class member receives a strip of paper.

2. A volunteer or the leader reads the directions aloud, pausing to allow the class members to follow each direction as it is read.

   a. Hold the paper strip vertically.

   b. Fold the top over to approximately one and one half inches from the bottom.

   c. Crease the paper at the fold.

   d. Open the strip and hold it vertically again.

   e. From the top, tear the strip down the middle, just to the crease, creating two flaps.

   f. Fold one flap forward and one flap back.

   g. Crease the flaps at the fold and let the flaps loose.

   h. One quarter inch below the crease tear the strip on either side toward the middle. Leave one quarter to one half inch attached in the middle.

   i. Fold the sides of the bottom of the strip toward the middle so that one side overlaps the other creating a stem.

   j. Fold the bottom of the stem up three quarters of an inch.

   k. Stand up, hold the strip up vertically by the stem.

   l. Let it go.

3. Process this activity by answering the following questions:

   a. What was the content you listened for in this activity?

   b. Give examples of other times you might listen for content.

   c. What might happen if you did not focus your attention on content in this activity?

   d. What might happen if you did not focus your attention on content when you are listening to a friend?

Activity 33
Body Communication

Purpose:

To show how different parts of the body communicate non-verbal messages.

Materials:

None

Procedure:

1. In a small group, make a list of body parts that communicate messages. For example, the hands, fingers.

2. Discuss with your group the different messages these body parts send. For example, the hands can "say" good-bye.

3. With your group, choose a message from the list below and demonstrate it for the rest of the class using only the appropriate body parts. Note: Each group should choose a different message.

   "I like you."

   "You made a mistake."

   "Go away."

   "I'm angry at you."

   "Come on, join the group."

4. Brainstorm as a class other messages that can be communicated with your body parts.

5. Discuss as a class the body parts that were used. How many did you find? How clear were the messages? What happens when messages are misread?

Activity 34
Looking for a Listener

Purpose:

To experience the feelings of being listened to and of being ignored.

Materials:

Small slips of paper

Procedure:

1. On individual slips of paper, print the following instructions:
   a. Don't look up.
   b. Read a book.
   c. Start talking about your own problems.
   d. Change the subject.
   e. Yawn and look bored.

   Do as many slips of paper as you have class members, giving the same instructions more than once.

   For example, if there are 12 class members, you would write, "Don't look up" on two slips of paper, "Read a book" on two slips, and so forth.

2. A volunteer becomes the first peer to look for a listener.

3. Each class member receives a slip of paper with an instruction on it.

4. The volunteer thinks of something important or interesting that happened recently. The volunteer tells six other students what happened.

5. Follow the instructions on your slip of paper if the volunteer tries to talk to you.

6. As many class members as possible should have an opportunity to be the volunteer.

7. Discuss as a class how it felt to be ignored.

8. Discuss what you wanted to do or say when no one would listen to you.

9. Following the procedure in the first part of this activity, write the following instructions on individual slips of paper:

    a. Lean forward toward the speaker.

    b. Make and keep eye contact. (Do not stare.)

    c. Look at the person and nod your head or smile.

    d. Say things that will let the speaker know you are listening. For example: I see, oh really, uh huh.

    e. Ask an open question such as, "What else happened?"

    All class members should receive a slip of paper.

10. Discuss with your class how it felt to have someone's attention.

11. Recall a situation when you really felt the other person was listening to you.

Activity 35
Name That Tune

Purpose:

To understand the need to pay attention to verbal and non-verbal clues when listening.

Materials:

Cassette, CD, or record player

Procedure:

1. At home, write a few phrases from your favorite song and bring them to class along with a recording of the song, if you have it.

2. With your class, take turns reading the phrases aloud and allowing the class members to guess the name of the songs.

3. Play the song after the class members have guessed the name.

4. As a class, discuss the difficulty of recognizing a song without hearing the music.

5. If we have to hear both the words and the music to easily recognize a song, what do we have to pay attention to in order to truly understand what a person is saying?

Activity 36

The Tiger Lake Tale

Purpose:

To practice attentive listening by paying attention to the speaker, following the ideas of the speaker, thinking about what is being said, and tuning out any distractions.

Materials:

None

Procedure:

1. The class should sit in one row or a half circle.

2. A volunteer or the leader reads *The Tiger Lake Tale*. The reader should sit facing the class and should pause at each blank in the story.

3. At each pause, a student will fill in the blank by calling out the appropriate word from the word list.

4. Begin at one end of the row, with each student filling in a blank until the whole story is told. If everyone has had a turn and the story is not finished, start over again.

   For example:

   If the story began "Mary had a little —" and the word list was: barn, kite, white, lamb, black, and boy, the first student in the row would call out "lamb." With fleece as—as snow, the second student in the row would call out "white."

5. When the story is complete, discuss the following questions.

   a. Was it more difficult to find the right word at the beginning or at the end of the story? Why?

   b. If you listened to this story on a playground with other students around, what would change?

   c. Did the reader help you to follow the story in any way?

Word List

sun	water	zebra	perfect
tree	pizza	names	crazy
cups	grass	hill	ran
poodle	shoes	frogs	hopped
Saturday	frisbee	windows	watched
lemonade	toes	Honda	bang
jellybeans	towel	home	threw
house	basket	brown	light
cheese	hour	grass	
video store	lake	blue	
door	hoot	sour	
ham	flashlights	scared	
worms	sand	golden	
tail	slimy	lost	

The Tiger Lake Tale

It was a beautiful day. The _____ shone brightly in a deep _____ sky. Best of all, it was _____ and there was no school.

Tanya called good-bye to her mother, picked up her backpack, and rushed out of the _____, slamming the _____ behind her. Her old _____ retriever wagged his _____ at her as she _____ by. Not long ago he would have followed Tanya down the street, but now he just _____ her go and then looked for a place on the cool _____ to rest.

Tanya hurried along. She was meeting Scott and Angela and they were all walking to Tiger Lake for a picnic. The two were waiting for her on the corner and off they went. Tanya's backpack was full of sandwiches. Angela carried a big thermos and a _____ to toss around after lunch. Scott had a _____ with chips and pickles in it.

It took them over an _____ to get to the _____ and several more minutes to find the _____spot. They spread a _____ in the shade of a large _____right next to the sparkling water. It was too early in the year for swimming so they took off their _____ to wade in the cool water.

Then they sat down to eat. Tanya had made wonderful _____ and _____ sandwiches. Angela poured _____ into paper _____. Scott opened a jar of very ____ pickles. They were starved and it all tasted delicious.

After they finished eating, they decided to go exploring. Hidden behind some bushes, they discovered a small beach and wrote their names with a stick in the soft _____. They climbed a _____ and peered in the _____ of an old empty house they found there. They splashed about in a small stream that fed into the lake.

Then, suddenly, it was time to go. They realized they had walked a long way around the lake, and quickly they started back the way they had come. The bushes seemed thicker and more difficult to get through than before, and nothing seemed familiar. It was nearly dark when Tanya, Angela, and Scott realized they were _____.

Now, they were really _____, but decided to stay where they were until it was _____ again. The three huddled together to wait. The only noises were the _____ of an owl and the croaking of _____ in the lake. It seemed as if hours had passed when they heard a different noise, distant at first and then much closer. Someone was calling their _____.

"Scott! Angela! Tanya!"

"We're here," they called, and suddenly the beams from _____ shone in their faces. The familiar voices of their parents surrounded them.

They were headed for home!

61

Activity 37
How Do You Feel About...?

Purpose:

To practice asking open and closed questions.

Materials:

None

Procedure:

1. Find a partner. Decide who will be partner A and who will be partner B.

2. Partner A begins by asking the questions from the question list. Partner B answers each question in his or her own way.

3. After all questions have been asked and answered, reverse. Partner B asks the questions and partner A answers.

4. As a class, discuss the following questions:

    a. Which questions got the most detailed answers?

    b. When would you want to ask a closed question?

    c. If you needed directions, which kind of question would you ask?

Question List

1. Do you like school?

2. What's your favorite subject?

3. Tell me about the best vacation you ever had.

4. How do you feel about the amount of homework you have this year?

5. What do you think would happen if our school schedule was changed and summer vacation started in July?

Activity 38
Practice Practice

Purpose:

To practice the skills that you learned in this chapter outside the classroom.

Materials:

None

Procedure:

1. Find two people in your school to listen to, using your verbal and non-verbal listening skills.

2. When you return to Peer Listening Class, discuss the following questions:

   a. Which listening skills did you use?

   b. What kinds of problems were shared with you? (Do not use real names.)

   c. Did you ask any questions? What were they?

   d. Did you run into difficulties? What were they?

Activity 39
Looking at My Skills

Purpose:

To summarize and evaluate the skills that you learned in this chapter.

Materials:

None

Procedure:

1. On this page, write how you feel about your level of skill as a Peer Listener.

2. Include some reflection on your practice experience.

   a. What happened that made you proud?

   b. What would you do differently next time?

   c. In what areas do you need improvement?

My Reflections:

_____

_____

_____

_____

_____

_____

_____

Chapter VI
Listening for Feelings

Be sure to look for...

❏ **A Red Face**

❏ **Saying Goodbye to a Friend**

❏ **Jealous Feelings**

Feelings

If you listen carefully, you will discover there are feelings behind the words you hear. When you are able to identify those feelings or clarify them, the person you are listening to knows you understand. Also, you know you have done a good job of listening.

For example, if someone says to you, "I won! I won!" you would probably identify the feelings that person was experiencing as excitement or happiness. To clarify those feelings, you might say to that person, "You must be excited" or "You sound happy."

Clarifying can also be a restatement of the feelings someone has expressed. For example, if someone says to you, "I am so angry," you could clarify that person's feelings by saying, "You seem very angry."

Everyone has feelings and those feelings are neither right nor wrong. They are simply your personal way of responding to and understanding life. No one can tell anyone else how to feel or change someone else's feelings. Have you ever had someone say to you, "Don't be mad" when you were very angry? Accepting the feelings of others is an important part of Peer Listening.

Opinions and Beliefs

Being prepared to hear things that you disagree with or that go against your value system is also important. Unlike feelings, opinion and beliefs can be changed, but that is not the job of a Peer Listener.

If you are listening to something that makes you very uncomfortable, you can tell the person to whom you are listening to find another Peer Listener. For example, if someone wants to talk to you about how great it is to smoke cigarettes and you hate smoking and begin to feel uncomfortable, you can say "I can't listen right now. I think you should talk to Mike or Susan."

Most important of all when listening for feelings is to be able to recognize your own feelings. You have to know and accept your own feelings before you can recognize and understand the feelings of others.

Activity 40
I Feel

Purpose:

To identify your feelings in order to better understand the feelings of others.

Materials:

None

Procedure:

1. Divide into small groups and form small group circles. Each member should have a copy of the *I Feel...* statements.

2. Beginning with the first statement, go around the group, each person having an opportunity to complete the statement aloud. Group members have the right to pass at any time. There should be no comments made during the exercise.

3. When all of the group members have had a chance to respond to all of the statements, discuss the following questions as a class:

   a. What was hard about this exercise?

   b. How did you feel about completing the first statements? Did it get easier?

   c. Did your group help you feel comfortable about making your statements? If so, how?

I Feel...

1. I am happiest when _____

2. People can usually tell when I'm feeling good because ____
   _____

3. When I'm lonely, I usually _____

4. If I get really mad about something, I _____

5. People can or cannot tell when I'm mad because I _____
   _____

6. When someone compliments or praises me, I feel _____
   _____

7. I get scared when _____

8. I sometimes wish I was _____

9. I am jealous of people who _____

10. I need other people because _____

11. Other people need me because _____

Activity 41
The Color of Feelings

Purpose:

To understand how we experience feelings in our minds and bodies.

Materials:

Newsprint or large paper, magic markers

Procedure:

1. With your small group, make a list of feeling words, both pleasant and unpleasant. For example, happy, sad, and angry are all feeling words.

2. Discuss with your group what color you think of when you see those feeling words. Why do you think of these colors? For example, angry is red because your face gets flushed when you get angry.

3. With your group, draw an outline of a person on newsprint and color the parts of the body affected by different feelings. Be sure to use the color associated with that feeling. For example, you would put the color red on the face of your outline to represent a face flushed with anger.

4. Find a partner and try experiencing the feelings in the following statements.

    a. "I'm so mad I could scream."

    b. "I don't feel like talking to anyone today. I'll just sit alone and feel bad."

    c. "I'm really scared!"

    d. "Hooray! We won the game."

5. With your class, discuss how successful you were at feeling the feelings. Was it helpful to think of feelings as colors?

Activity 42

Facts and Feelings

Purpose:

To explore the difference between fact and feelings in the spoken message.

Materials:

None

Procedure:

1. A volunteer reads aloud each of the statements on the following page one at a time.

2. After each statement is read, underline the facts in the statements.

3. Write the word or two beside each statement that you believe describes the feelings of the speaker.

4. Discuss the following questions about the statements with your class.

   a. Did everyone agree on the facts in each statement?

   b. Was it difficult to identify the feelings?

   c. In which statements did the class members disagree on the kinds of feelings being expressed?

   d. Why do you think this happened?

Statements

"I wish it would snow tomorrow so I wouldn't have to take that math test."

"I'm going to Florida on vacation!"

"I have never told anyone that I have to wear a back brace at night."

"Only two more days until the dance!"

"My grandmother died."

"I saw James talking to another girl!"

"What if we get caught?"

"She took my book without asking."

"I made the team!"

Activity 43
Best Friends

Purpose:

To practice listening for feelings as well as content.

Materials:

None

Procedure:

1. A volunteer or the leader reads the following story to the class:

   Patsy Walker and I lived on the same street. I was born here and Patsy moved in when we were both four years old.

   We did everything together. We camped out in our back yards and even built a tree house in the woods that some other kids are using now.

   Last summer we rode our bikes to the pool every single day. We slept over at each others house and watched late night movies on TV. We both liked boys who were friends so all four of us would talk on the phone. We had the greatest summer and we had made all kinds of plans for school starting.

   And then Patsy moved! It happened really fast. One day she told me her dad's office was moving to New York and that same day the for sale sign went up in front of her house. One week later she was gone. Her parents wanted her to be in New York for the start of school.

   It didn't seem real when we said good-bye, but every time I looked at her house, I'd get an aching feeling in my stomach.

   The first day of school was awful. I cried that day when I got home and every day after that for a week.

   It's been six months now since Patsy moved. I met some kids on the bus that live two streets away. I still miss Patsy, but I'm having fun with my new friends.

2. Answer the following questions individually:

    a. How old were these girls when they first became friends?

    b. How did they meet?

    c. What did they do for fun when they were little?

    d. Where did they go on their bikes?

    e. What TV shows did they like to watch?

    f. Why did Patsy move?

    g. How did the friend feel about Patsy?

    h. How did the friend feel about Patsy's moving?

    i. What kind of feelings did she have when she looked at Patsy's house?

    j. What feelings are expressed most often in the story?

    k. How does the friend feel six months after Patsy moved?

    l. Has this ever happened to you? How did you feel?

3. As a class, discuss the difference between listening for *content* and listening for *feelings*.

4. Go back to the list of questions and identify content questions.

5. As a class, discuss why listening for feelings, not just content, is important.

Activity 44
Practice Practice

Purpose:

To practice the skills learned that you in this chapter outside the classroom.

Materials:

None

Procedure:

1. Keep a record of all of the feelings you have during one day at school.

2. When you return to your Peer Listening Class, share your list of feelings and discuss the following questions:

   a. What examples can you give of a feeling you had during the day? What were you doing? Who was with you? Why do you think you had the feeling?

   b. What was the most common feeling you had during the day?

   c. What was the most common feeling of the class as a whole?

   d. Did anything unusual happen during the day? If so, did it cause unusual feelings?

Activity 45

Looking at My Skills

Purpose:

To summarize and evaluate the skills that you learned in this chapter.

Materials:

None

Procedure:

1. On this page, write how you feel about your level of skill in listening for feelings.

2. Include some reflection on your practice experience.

   a. Of what feelings did you become more aware?

   b. What feelings make you most uncomfortable?

   c. How does understanding your own feelings help you understand others?

My Reflections:

_____

_____

_____

_____

_____

_____

_____

_____

_____

Chapter VII
Responding

Be sure to look for...

❑ **My Math Teacher Hates Me**

❑ **Giving Advice**

❑ **Refer to an Adult Immediately**

Have you ever had a friend tell you what you should or ought to do about something? Maybe your friend told you to cut your hair because she liked it better short. Perhaps your friend told you what to do to solve a problem you were having at home. How did you feel when that happened? Did you take your friend's advice?

Advice giving is one way people try to impose their beliefs and values on others. Because each person's values and beliefs are different, advice giving can be a way of trying to change what a person thinks or believes. Although the person giving the advice feels pretty important and truly wants to help, the person getting the advice doesn't feel important at all.

In fact, the person getting the advice may feel misunderstood, resentful, or even stupid! Most people want to control their own lives and make their own decisions. They also want other people to think they are capable of making decisions and solving problems.

Why then do people like to talk to someone when they have a problem? For support! For understanding! For feedback! And because talking about a problem sometimes helps the person to solve his or her own problem.

There are many ways to respond to what you will hear as a Peer Listener. Some responses help the speaker to continue sharing; other responses discourage or stop the sharing.

Checking for feelings lets the speaker know you are "tuned in" to the feelings behind the words. The response when you are checking for feelings is, "Sounds like you are feeling (name the feeling)."

Clarifying is a response that restates what the speaker has said. It lets the speaker know you understand what has been said. A clarifying response is, "Are you saying that (restate what the speaker said)?"

A pacifying response denies the feelings of the speaker and minimizes what is being said. An example of a pacifying response is, "Don't feel that way. Everything will be all right."

A put down response criticizes the speaker for what that person is saying and feeling. An example of a put down response is, "What a stupid thing to say."

Advising is another response that minimizes what the speaker is saying. An example of an advising response is, "Go outside. It's a beautiful day and you'll feel better."

If you read this section carefully, you will see that the two best responses a Peer Listener can use are clarifying and checking for feelings.

Activity 46

Not So Nice Advice

Purpose:

To understand why Peer Listeners don't give advice or tell others what to do.

Materials:

None

Procedure:

1. Find a partner. Decide which of you will have the problem (partner A) and which will give advice (partner B).

2. Partner A tells partner B about something that is of concern. Partner A can use a personal experience or choose from the list below.

3. Partner B tells partner A what should be done about the problem.

4. Partner A should respond the way the advice makes you feel. Example, partner A says, "I'm so worried about math. I failed the last test and we have another test on Tuesday. I just don't understand it." Partner B says, "You should study more and you ought to ask your father to help you. Fathers are good at math." Partner A then says, "I do study, and my father travels. He's only home on weekends."

5. As a class, discuss the feelings that partner A had about partner B's advice in the example.

6. All of the partner As in the class now answer the following questions about their partners' advice:

   a. Did the advice make sense for you?

   b. Was it something you were able to do?

   c. Was it something you wanted to do?

   d. How did you feel about yourself when you were being told what to do?

7. Partners reverse roles and repeat the activity. Suggestions for the role play:

   a. You have to baby-sit with your brother Friday night. Your friends are going to a movie.

   b. You don't like the way you look. You're not sure why.

   c. You are worried about a book report that's due next Monday. You haven't read the book yet.

   d. You want to try out for the basketball team, but you are not as tall as most of the players.

Activity 47
Red Light/Green Light

Purpose:

To learn to identify which problems can be listened to and which problems should be referred.

Materials:

Red, yellow, and green paper or cards

Procedure:

1. Each small group should have one sheet each of red, yellow, and green paper.

2. A volunteer or the leader reads the situations aloud to the class.

3. After each situation is read, decide with your group how the situation should be handled.

4. Vote as a group by holding up the appropriate color paper. GREEN means the situation calls for listening and nothing more. YELLOW means the situation can be listened to but may also need to be referred to an adult. RED means the situation should be referred to an adult immediately. For example, Situation: John tells you he had an argument with his friend. Your group decides that this situation can be handled by listening. Your group holds up a green card.

5. Discuss as a class the reasons groups voted differently in some situations.

6. With your class, think of some other situations that might come up when you are listening and discuss whether they are red, yellow, or green light situations.

Situations

- Kim comes to you because she's nervous about trying out for the softball team.

- Charlie comes to you very angry. Some older boys threw rocks at him on his way to school.

- Jay tells you his parents are getting a divorce.

- William tells you his father threw him down the stairs last night. He also tells you it was no big deal... that he wasn't hurt at all.

- Michelle comes to you because she's afraid her parents won't let her go to the football game with her friends.

- Sandra tells you her girlfriend has a wine cooler in her book bag and wants Sandra to try some with her after school.

- Sam tells you his locker mate takes up all the space in the locker.

- Jennifer comes to you because she likes a boy who won't pay any attention to her.

- Sharon tells you her mother won't let her talk on the phone for two weeks because she failed her math test.

- Deidre tells you she is going to run away because her parents are so mean to her.

- Maryann comes crying to you that she thinks she may be pregnant.

Activity 48

The Best Response

Purpose:

To practice responding.

Materials:

None

Procedure:

1. On your own, read the first five statements and responses and check the best one or two responses to each statement.

2. Read the second five statements and write your own best response to each.

3. Review the activity with your class. Discuss any statements that you had difficulty responding to.

Practice Sheet

1. I'm feeling so depressed...
   - ❑ a. Oh, don't feel sad.
   - ❑ b. You are telling me you have been depressed.
   - ❑ c. Are you crazy or something?
   - ❑ d. Sounds to me like you are really down and blue.
   - ❑ e. Go for a bike ride. You'll feel better.

2. They let a girl on a boy's baseball team. We're ruined!
   - ❑ a. Sounds to me like you are really upset.
   - ❑ b. Go to the coach and tell him you won't play if she does.
   - ❑ c. You are a male chauvinist.
   - ❑ d. Don't be upset. She probably won't last.
   - ❑ e. Are you saying you are upset about a girl that is going to play on your baseball team?

3. I have been smoking with my friends. I hope my mother doesn't find out.
   - ❑ a. Don't smoke, it's bad for you.

❑ b. Sounds like you are worried that your mother may find out that you have been smoking.

❑ c. Don't worry. Most parents don't care that much if their kids smoke.

❑ d. Only a stupid person would ever smoke.

❑ e. Are you saying you are scared that your mother will find out that you smoke?

4. Guess what! I've been nominated for the student council!

❑ a. Are you saying that you are going to run for student council?

❑ b. Be sure the teachers support you or you'll never get in.

❑ c. Anyone can get nominated for student council. It's no big deal.

❑ d. That's very nice. Maybe you'll get voted in.

❑ e. Sounds like you are excited.

5. I got my hair cut yesterday and it's too short!

❑ a. It really looks fine.

❑ b. Next time go to the person I go to.

❑ c. You look almost bald.

❑ d. Sounds like you're disappointed with your haircut.

❑ e. You're telling me you don't like your new haircut.

6. I think I just failed an English test.
Response: _____

7. Our class gets less time for lunch than others. It's not fair!
Response: _____

8. My friends and I tried some beer this weekend. It was fun!
Response: _____

9. I can't believe it! I got the lead in the school play!
Response: _____

10. My friend told me everyone laughs at my accent.
Response: _____

Activity 49
Response Rally

Purpose:

To practice appropriate responses.

Materials:

Magic markers, paper

Procedure:

1. Three to five volunteers are judges and sit in the front of the room. Each judge has four sheets of paper with the numbers 3, 2, 1, and 0 in large print on individual sheets.

2. The rest of the class is divided into two teams.

3. A volunteer or the leader reads the statements.

4. As the statements are read, each team decides on the best response and one team member reads the response aloud.

5. Judges award points according to the following scale:

   3   best response

   2   second best response

   1   poor response

   0   bad response

6. Write the points awarded each team on the board. The highest score wins.

Statements

1. My friends all went to the movies Friday night and they didn't invite me.
2. My mother comes in to clean my room. It's my room and she should ask!
3. We won and I made the winning basket!
4. I smoke a lot. It's fun.
5. My math teacher hates me.
6. My parents won't let me go to the game with my friends.
7. My boyfriend broke up with me.
8. My parents want to chaperon my party. I'll be so embarrassed.
9. I can't get my locker open.
10. I would really like to sleep on Saturday morning. I don't want to go to soccer practice any more.

Sandra Peyser Hazouri and Miriam Frey Smith

Activity 50
Practice Practice

Purpose:

To practice the skills that you learned in this chapter outside the classroom.

Materials:

None

Procedure:

1. Find two people in your school to listen to using your listening *and* responding skills.

2. When you return to your Peer Listening Class, discuss the following questions:

   a. What kind of problems were shared with you? (Do not use real names.)

   b. Which responding skills did you use?

   c. What was the most difficult part of responding?

Activity 51

Looking at My Skills

Purpose:

To summarize and evaluate the skills that you learned in this chapter.

Materials:

None

Procedure:

1. On this page, write how you feel about your level of skill in responding.

2. Include some reflection on your practice experience.

   a. Of what were you most proud?

   b. What will you do differently next time?

   c. In what area do you need improvement?

My Reflections:

_____

_____

_____

_____

_____

_____

_____

_____

Chapter VIII
Taking Care
of the Listener

Be sure to look for...

❑ **Invisible Fences**

❑ **Enabling a Friend**

❑ **Can I Borrow Your Book?**

Setting Limits

Listening to others is not an easy task. While you're listening, you have to put aside your own feelings and concerns in order to focus on the feelings and problems of the other person. In a way, you are taking care of the other person by listening. It is important for you as a Peer Listener to take care of yourself as well.

Setting limits to how helpful you will be is one way of taking care of yourself. Always remembering that the problems people share with you are their problems will help you to avoid taking on those problems as if they were yours. Not allowing other people to interfere with what you want or need to do will help you to keep control of your listening activities and your life.

Sometimes saying no to the requests or desires of others will help. Also, learning how to call on an adult when you encounter situations that are uncomfortable or worrisome will help. This way you can get the support you need when life is stressful and the problem is beyond your knowledge or skill level.

Enabling

People that are in a position to help others can overdo it. Over helping means doing for others what they can do for themselves. *Enabling* is another word for over helping. When you enable others, you take on their responsibilities, stand between them and the consequences of their mistakes, and make decisions for them. Enabling sometimes eases a problem for the moment, but it never solves the problem.

For example, giving someone the answers to a test enables the person to pass this test, but it doesn't solve the problem of not studying. It is important for Peer Listeners to allow others to experience the consequences of their actions. Showing concern for others and supporting their positive efforts is true helping.

Group Identity

You are learning a great deal about the importance of caring for yourself and for others. It is also important that you take care of your Peer Listening Group. One of the ways you can do this by giving you group an identity with a logo that can be easily recognized by your fellow students.

A logo is a symbol. It stands for or represents something else. Logos are usually designs or pictures which are often in distinct colors and sometimes combined with words or initials. Logos are used to represent every kind of organization or product to help them to stand out from all others. For example, the North Carolina Peer Helper Association has as its logo three figures in a circle, arms connected, standing on an outline of the state of North Carolina. The initials NCPHA are part of the logo.

Your logo will remind you of all you have learned and will tell others what Peer Listeners are all about.

Activity 52
A Logo for Listeners

Purpose:

To create a logo that symbolizes what you stand for as a group of Peer Listeners.

Materials:

Newsprint or poster board, magic markers

Procedure:

1. In your small groups, brainstorm ideas for logos by answering the following questions. If the class is small, work as a single group throughout this exercise.

   a. What is the purpose of our Peer Listening Group?

   b. What are some characteristics of Peer Listeners?

   c. What are some pictures that could symbolize these characteristics? For example, a picture of a heart can symbolize love.

   d. Does your group have a special name that could be symbolized in the logo? For example, PAL is a special name for a Peer Listening Group called Peers Are Listening.

   e. Does your school or organization have special colors that you could use in your logo?

2. As a class, list the small group ideas on the board under the following headings:

   PURPOSE   CHARACTERISTICS

   SYMBOLS   NAMES   COLORS

3. After all the ideas have been listed, vote as a class on each idea. Circle the idea under each heading that gets the most votes.

Sandra Peyser Hazouri and Miriam Frey Smith

4. Return to your small group and on newsprint sketch out a logo by combining the ideas circled on the board.

5. Share your group's logo idea with the class. Applaud everyone's efforts.

6. Vote as a class on the logo that most clearly represents your Peer Listening Group.

7. Begin using your logo on announcements, notices, brochures, T shirts, and posters so the logo becomes associated with your group.

Activity 53
Finding Your Personal Space

Purpose:

To experience the boundaries that mark your personal space.

Materials:

None

Procedure:

1. Find a partner.

2. Stand in the center of the room, away from the furniture, facing your partner.

3. Keep in eye contact with your partner.

4. Remain standing in the center of the room while your partner backs up to the wall.

5. Remain standing in the center while your partner, keeping eye contact, walks slowly toward you as close as possible.

6. Reverse roles with your partner.

7. Discuss with the class the feelings you had as your partner moved closer and closer. Was there a time when you wanted to say, "Far enough?" Did you want to put your hand up to stop that person? Did you want to back up at some point because your partner was too close? Chances are you had some kind of discomfort as your partner began to get close. That discomfort was a signal that your partner had invaded your personal space or had come too close to your space. If this was not an exercise where you were following instructions, it would be important for you to let your partner know where your boundaries are by stepping back, putting up your hand and saying, "Far enough."

8. Discuss with your group other ways people invade your personal space.

Activity 54
The Sean Story

Purpose:

To understand how helping can sometimes enable someone to keep making the same mistakes.

Materials:

None

Procedure:

1. A volunteer or the leader follows directions and reads "I'm Sean" aloud to the class. A Boy is chosen to stand at the front of the class as Sean. As each character in the story is introduced, another class member is chosen to represent that character.

2. As the characters come to the front of the class, they should stand on either side of Sean and behind him. Sean should be able to lean against them in a relaxed fashion. (Students will need to be directed to these positions.)

3. At the PAUSE in the story, Sean should be comfortably surrounded and supported by the characters in the story. Ask Sean how he feels with all these people supporting him.

4. Continue reading the story, asking each character to go back to a seat at the appropriate time. At the end of the story, Sean should be standing alone. Ask Sean how he feels now. Thank Sean and applaud all of the characters.

5. As a class, answer the following questions:

   a. What were Sean's family and friends doing?

   b. What happened to Sean when everyone was supporting him?

   c. Can you think of a time when you enabled someone to keep making the same mistake?

"I'm Sean"

I'm Sean. I'm twelve years old and I'm in the seventh grade. I really like shooting baskets with my friend Mike and playing in the City Soccer League. School's okay too, I guess. Except for the homework—especially the projects! I don't spend a lot of time on projects like some other kids do. I've got more important things to do.

This is my mom. She is always helping me out. Last time I had a project assignment, I forgot about it. Mom went out the night before it was due to get poster paper for me. She's great.

This is my dad. He brought all the magic markers home from the office for me to use.... It's against the office rules to do that, but he said he wanted to help me out. What a terrific dad.

This is my little sister, Penny. Penny is better than I am at drawing, so she did the pictures for my project. She's okay.

This is Mike. He's my best friend. Mike does great projects and he's always finishing when I'm just starting. The last few times we've had projects, Mike came over and helped me after his project was finished. Mike's a good friend.

This is my teacher, Mrs. Miller. I've had to call her at home a few times when I've forgotten the instructions for a project assignment. She doesn't mind at all. She's a very nice person.

PAUSE

Today my teacher reminded me that we have a project due tomorrow. She said that we should all be finishing up by now. Then she took me aside and said I was not to disturb her at home again. And I thought she was so nice!

I asked my friend Mike when he would be over. He said he had his own stuff to finish and he wouldn't be able to help me! Some friend.

Penny was getting ready to leave for a scout meeting when I got home. I said I'd let her wear my soccer jacket for a week if she would help me. She said she would rather go to scouts.

I called Dad and he said he was sorry but he didn't feel good about borrowing office supplies. He said I'd have to make do with Penny's crayons. Crayons! Nobody does projects with crayons!

Mom told me no when I asked her to get me some project paper. She said she was a busy person, and if I needed her to do something, I should ask in time for her to fit it into her schedule.

Now what am I going to do?

Activity 55

Circles

Purpose:

To become more comfortable using the word "no."

Materials:

None

Procedure:

1. Line up with your class in an open area.

2. Count off by 2s.

3. All number ones form a circle. All number twos form a circle around the number ones.

4. Face someone in the opposite circle.

5. Circle one thinks of something each might ask of a friend. For example, "Can I borrow your science book?" or "Can I have a ride home today?" or "Will you help me after school?" Circle two thinks of a firm way to say no. For example, "No, I can't." "No, sorry." "No, maybe another time."

6. Circle ones, begin with the person you are facing and ask for what you want. Then, moving to the right, ask each person in circle two the same question. Circle two, stand still and say "No" in your own way to each person in circle one as he or she comes by. (If your group is small, go around twice).

7. After circle one is back where it started, reverse. Circle two will ask for something and move around circle one. Circle one will stand still and say "No."

8. With your class, discuss the following questions:

   a. When was it most difficult to say no, at the beginning of the exercise or at the end? Why?

   b. Was it easier or harder to say no to someone you knew well? Why?

   c. Have you had an experience when you wanted or needed to say "No" but didn't? What happened? How did you feel?

Activity 56

An Unusual Day in the Life of a Peer Listener

Purpose:

To understand when confidential information should be shared with a responsible adult.

Materials:

None

Procedure:

1. With your class, select volunteers to play the parts. All other students will be the chorus.

2. Rehearse the plays once and then perform them.

3. After each play, discuss with your class the way a Peer Listener might feel when her or she realized that an adult had to be told.

4. Discuss why the Peer Listener in each play felt it was necessary to tell an adult.

Sandra Peyser Hazouri and Miriam Frey Smith

Paul's Problem

Characters:

Narrator	Paul
Ms. Wilson, teacher	Mike, Peer Listener

Narrator: As the scene opens, Paul is standing in the school hall holding his books.

Ms. Wilson, the teacher, enters from the right.

Ms. W: Good morning, Paul. Why, you look tired this morning!

Paul: Hey, Ms. Wilson. I'm okay. Up kinda late last night is all.

Ms. W: Well, I hope it was because you were studying for my test. I'll see you at 11:00.

Ms. Wilson exits to the left. Mike enters from the right.

Paul: Mike! Come 'ere! I need a favor. Hand me your notes. I need to study for Ms. Wilson's test.

Mike: Paul, my notes won't do you any good now. You've got a class. Why didn't you study last night?

Paul: I'll tell you but you have to promise you won't tell.

Chorus: *(chant together softly)*

Shhh, Shhh, Shhh, Don't tell!

Shhh, Shhh, Shhh, Don't tell!

Mike: Paul, I'm a Peer Listener. If you tell me something that's gonna hurt you or anyone else, I gotta tell.

Paul: Yea yea. Anyway, I drank beer with some high school guys last night. I had so much I don't even remember how I got home. That happens a lot!

Mike: You mean you've done it before?

Paul: All the time! This guy lives on my street and his dad works the night shift so I go there with some other guys and drink beer. Mom thinks he's helping me study.

Chorus: *(chant softly)*

You gotta tell an adult.

You gotta tell an adult.

Mike: We've got to go to class now Paul. Let's talk some more later.

Chorus: *(chant louder)*

You've gotta tell an adult.

You've gotta tell an adult.

Chorus: *(chant very loud)*

You've gotta tell an adult

Mike: *(turning to the audience)*

I've gotta tell an adult.

Joan Feels Alone

Characters:

Narrator	Kim
Joan	Sandy, Peer Listener

Narrator: As the scene opens, Joan is sitting by herself on the bleachers at _____ Middle School.

Kim and Sandy enter from the right.

Kim: Joanie, where have you been? We've been looking for you Everybody's going to my house after school.... Wanna come?

Joan: No thanks, I can't.

Kim: *(angry)*

Joanie, you never want to do anything with us! You act like you're too good for us or something.

Kim stomps out! Sandy sits down beside Joan.

Joan: Sandy, I'm not snubbing her... honest! It's just that my parents are really strict. I'm never allowed to do anything.

Sandy: That must be hard.

Joan: I can hardly stand it! Don't tell anyone, but I'm thinking of running away.

Chorus: *(softly)*

Shh, Shh, Shh.

Don't tell.

Shh, Shh, Shh.

Don't tell.

Sandy: Joanie, you know I'm a Peer Listener. If you tell me anything that may harm you or anyone else, I have to tell an adult.

Joan: Please don't tell! I've got some money my grandfather gave me and I've already called the bus station about tickets.

Chorus: *(softly)*

You gotta tell an adult.

You gotta tell an adult.

Sandy: But Joanie, where would you go?

Joan: I shouldn't have said anything. I have to go home now... Please... don't tell.

Joan exits to the left.

Chorus: *(louder)*

You gotta tell an adult.

Chorus: *(very loud)*

You gotta tell an adult!

Sandy: *(looking at the audience)*

I've got to tell an adult.

Heather's Secret

Characters:

Narrator	Joe
Heather	Mary, Peer Listener

Narrator: As the scene opens, Heather and Joe are standing near a tree in the yard at _____ Middle School.

Joe: *(loudly)*

Then you figure it out Heather! I don't know what else to do.

Joe stomps out to the left. Heather watches him go and wipes her eyes. Mary enters from the right.

Mary: Heather, are you okay? You look like you have been crying.

Heather: Oh Mary! I'm in the biggest mess.

Mary: What is it?

Heather: You're a Peer Listener. You've got to keep everything confidential, right?

Chorus: *(softly)*

Shhh, Shhh, Shhh.

Don't tell.

Shh, Shhh, Shhh.

Don't tell.

Mary: Yes, I have to keep things confidential unless you tell me something that may harm you or others... then I have to tell an adult.

Heather: Mary, please! Promise me no matter what you won't tell this one time.

Mary: I can't promise.

Heather: Great! I'm in the worst trouble of my life and I've got no one to talk to.

Chorus: *(softly)*

You gotta tell an adult.

You gotta tell an adult.

Mary: Maybe you should talk to Mrs....

Heather: *(shouts)*

No! I'm not talking to anyone.

She runs out to the left.

Chorus: *(louder)*

You gotta tell an adult.

You gotta tell an adult.

Chorus: *(very loud)*

You gotta tell an adult.

Mary looks at the audience.

Mary: Heather's in some kind of trouble. I've gotta tell an adult.

Activity 57
Practice Practice

Purpose:

To practice the skills that you learned in this chapter outside the classroom.

Materials:

None

Procedure:

1. During the school day, practice saying no to requests from friends that interfere with your time, invade your space, or are things that they could do for themselves.

2. When you return to your Peer Listening Class, discuss the following questions:

   a. What were some of the requests?

   b. Was it difficult to say no without making your friends mad?

   c. How did you handle the situation?

   d. How can you say no *and* keep your friends?

Activity 58
Looking at My Skills

Purpose:

To summarize and evaluate the skills that you learned in this chapter.

Materials:

None

Procedure:

1. On this page, write how you feel about your level of skill in taking care of yourself.

2. Include some reflection on your practice experience.

   a. Of what were you most proud?

   b. What will you do differently next time?

   c. In what areas do you need improvement?

My Reflections:

_____

_____

_____

_____

_____

_____

_____

_____

Chapter IX
Making Choices

Be sure to look for...

❏ **Decision-Making Model**

❏ **Spending Twenty Dollars**

❏ **Puzzles**

After you have had lots of practice listening and responding, you may feel capable of helping a friend work through a problem or make a decision. Problem solving and decision making are skills like listening that must be learned and practiced. When you assist others with decision making and problem solving, you are helping them to learn these skills.

You have already learned that people need to feel capable. Giving advice, taking on others' problems, or telling others what to do robs them of the opportunity to feel capable of handling their lives. Helping others learn skills for coping with their lives is the appropriate role of the Peer Listener.

Define the problem

The first step in making a decision is figuring out what the problem is. Sometimes the real problem is hidden under many feelings or other concerns. For example, Yvonne may tell you that she hates her mother, or that her mother is unreasonable or mean. That information tells you a great deal about how Yvonne is feeling toward her mother but it does not identify the problem. Asking open questions and listening attentively will help to uncover the real issue. In this case it may be that Yvonne's mother wants her to go to her grandmother's house for the weekend and she will miss the school dance on Friday night. Missing the dance Friday night is the problem.

There may be another problem in this situation, such as poor communication with her mother, but you can only work on one problem at a time. Focus on one problem and get as many details as possible. Ask Yvonne what happened and when. Find out how long the problem has been going on and what has already been tried to resolve it.

Search for the alternatives

Once the problem is clearly identified, you can begin to figure out what to do about it. Instruct the person to think of as many alternatives as possible to solve this problem. These alternatives are the choices a person has in any situation. In Yvonne's case where she would miss the Friday night dance, there are several alternatives. She can do nothing and miss the dance, talk to her mother about going to her grandmother's house another time, or tell her mother she has to stay home and study for a big test that weekend.

Sometimes the person with the problem will not be able to think of any alternatives. As a Peer Listener, you may offer several possible choices to help the process. It is important to remember not to give the person a solution or in any way solve the problem by making the decision for the other person.

Look at the consequences

Every alternative has an outcome. Your next step is to help the person with the problem look at the consequences of each choice. The person will need to ask what will happen if I try this? What will happen if I choose that? Some alternatives will have all positive or all negative consequences, but most will have both. For example, if Yvonne chooses the alternative of doing nothing, she will experience the negative consequence of missing the dance and the positive consequence of pleasing her mother.

Choose the best alternative

Encourage the person with the problem to choose the alternative that has the most positive outcome and that is the most comfortable.

Act on your choice

Have the person make a commitment to take action on the choice by being specific as to when and how the decision will be implemented. It is important to make an appointment with the person for sometime after the choice has been acted upon.

Evaluate your choice

When you get back together, evaluate with the person how things went. Did he or she make the right choice? If the person is not satisfied with the outcome, choose another alternative and begin again.

Activity 59

Decisions, Decisions, Decisions

Purpose:

To practice the decision-making model.

Materials:

Decision-Making Model

Procedure:

1. Divide into small groups.

2. Each group takes one of the following decisions:

   a. Should I take algebra next year?

   b. Should I smoke cigarettes with my friends?

   c. Should I try out for the track team? My friends will think I'm a sissy.

   d. Should I be friends with the girl who sits next to me in English? No one seems to like her.

   e. Should I get a job this summer?

   f. I don't like my math teacher. Should I tell her off?

3. Using the *Decision-Making Model* presented on the following page, go through the steps to help a peer make a decision.

4. Have the groups explain their choices to the class.

5. Discuss the following questions:

   a. Could another alternative have been chosen?

   b. Would the outcome be the same?

   c. Should the Peer Listener make the decision for the student?

Decision-Making Model

Step I: Define the problem.

What is the problem?

Who owns the problem?

When did it happen?

Step II: Search for the alternatives.

Brainstorm all the possible solutions to the problems.

Step III: Look at the consequences.

What are the positive and negative

outcomes of each alternative?

Step IV: Choose the best alternative.

Pick the solution that best fits you.

Step V: Act on your choice.

Put your plan into action.

Step VI: Evaluate your choice.

Did your plan work well? If not, go back to step IV.

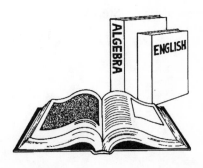

Activity 60
Puzzling Decisions

Purpose:

To learn that some decisions are harder to make than others.

Materials:

Two pieces of poster board, magic markers, scissors, and tape

Procedure:

1. A volunteer or the leader writes the following on the poster boards:

Poster Board #1 What should I wear today?

Step I:	Define the problem
Step II:	Search for the alternatives
Step III:	Look at the consequences
Step IV:	Choose the best alternative
Step V:	Act on your choice
Step VI:	Evaluate your choice

Poster Board #2 Should I smoke cigarettes?

Step I:	Define the problem
Step II:	Search for the alternatives
Step III:	Look at the consequences
Step IV:	Choose the best alternative
Step V:	Act on your choice
Step VI:	Evaluate your choice

2. Cut each poster in 10 or more pieces, depending on the size of the group.

3. Put the pieces in a paper bag and mix them up.

4. Distribute one piece to each class member. If there are left over pieces, lay them out on a desk at the front of the room.

5. With your class, find the other pieces that will put both poster boards back together. Be sure to check the extra pieces to complete the poster.

6. Tape the posters back together.

7. Divide into two groups, each one completing one of the decisions on the posters. Fill in the appropriate spaces as you go through the decision-making process.

8. Share your poster with the whole class and discuss the following:

   a. Did your group have an easy or difficult decision to make?

   b. Why was it easy or difficult?

   c. How many alternatives were there?

   d. Were there both positive and negative consequences?

   e. Why do you think some decisions are harder to make than others?

Activity 61
A Day at the Mall

Purpose:

To explore the decision-making process.

Materials:

None

Procedure:

1. Divide into small groups.

2. Read the problem below and decide with your group exactly how to spend $20.00. Everyone must agree.

3. Share with the class how your group decided to spend the money.

4. Share with the class how your group made decisions.

5. Discuss as a class the difficulties of making a group decision.

Problem

You and your friends are spending the day at the mall. You have $20.00 that was given to you for your birthday.

❑ You should probably buy a new shirt.

❑ Your friends want to play video games.

❑ You're hungry.

❑ There is a good movie playing.

❑ You need new sunglasses because you lost yours.

❑ Your best friend wants to borrow $5.00.

❑ You have a savings account for college.

❑ There is a sale on great looking shorts.

Activity 62

Using All Your Skills

Purpose:

To practice the skills that you learned in *Peer Listening in the Middle School.*

Materials:

None

Procedure:

1. With your class, form groups of three (triads).

2. In your triad, decide who will be the speaker, the Peer Listener, and the observer.

3. The speaker will choose one of the situations below to talk about.

4. The listener will use all of the Peer Listener skills while listening to the speaker. The listener will:

   a. Listen attentively using verbal and non-verbal listening skills

   b. Listen for feelings

   c. Check for feelings

   d. Use clarifying responses

   e. Take the speaker through the decision-making model

For example, the speaker says, "I don't know whether or not to go to the school dance." Listen attentively by looking at the person, leaning forward, keeping eye contact, nodding, asking an open question like, "How do you feel about going to the dance?" Listen for feelings by watching the other person, looking for the emotion behind the words. Check for feelings by saying something like, "Sounds like you are confused about whether or not to go to the dance." Clarify by saying something like you are trying to decide whether or not to go to the dance. Go through the decision-making model with the person by asking for alternatives, "What could he or she do instead of going to the dance?" "What would be the consequences of that choice?" "What would happen if he or she did go to the dance?"

5. The observer watches the Peer Listener and checks to see how well all the listening skills are used. The observer gives positive feedback and suggestions at the end of the activity.

6. Change roles so that each person in the triad has an opportunity to be the Peer Listener.

Situations

1. "It's getting close to the end of school and I'm not sure what to do this summer."

2. "My boyfriend is not calling me like he used to. What should I do?"

3. "Guess what! I got $50 for my birthday. I don't know what to spend it on though."

4. "There's going to be beer at the party. I don't know if I should go."

5. "I have to be home earlier than everybody else. It's not fair."

Activity 63
Practice Practice

Purpose:

To practice the skills that you learned in this chapter outside the classroom.

Materials:

None

Procedure:

1. Find two people in your school who have a problem or a decision to make and work with them through the decision-making model.

2. When you return to your Peer Listening Class, answer the following questions:

   a. What kind of problems were shared? (Do not use real names.)

   b. Were they easy to define?

   c. Was the person with the problem able to come up with alternatives?

   d. Was the person able to identify consequences for each alternative?

   e. Is the person putting his or her decision into action?

   f. When is your next meeting with the person?

   g. What were the difficulties you had with this activity?

Activity 64
Looking at My Skills

Purpose:

To summarize and evaluate the skills that you learned in this chapter.

Materials:

None

Procedure:

1. On this page, write how you feel about your level of skill in decision making.

2. Include some reflections on your practice experience.

   a. Of what were you most proud?

   b. What would you do differently next time?

   c. In what areas do you need improvement?

My Reflections:

_____

_____

_____

_____

_____

_____

_____

Chapter X
It's Official

Be sure to look for...

❑ **Your Own Certificate**

❑ **Practicing New Skills**

❑ **Applaud Each Other**

You have accomplished a great deal and learned many new skills during these past weeks. What you have learned will serve you well in dealing with your parents, teachers, and friends throughout your life. When you begin to interview for jobs or college, you can draw on your listening and responding skills. Decisions will be less difficult for you because you understand the process.

You have also learned to look at other people in a new way and with greater understanding. Acquaintances have become close friends in your Peer Listening Class and you have learned to reach out to new friends through Peer Listening Activities.

It is time to celebrate these accomplishments and applaud yourself for taking the risk to grow. You have done well!

Activity 65
Post Test: Peer Listening Inventory

Purpose:

To assess your Peer Listening Skills now that training is finished.

Materials:

The *Peer Listening Inventory* you took at the beginning of your Peer Listening Class and a blank copy of the *Peer Listening Inventory*

Procedure:

1. Take the *Peer Listening Inventory* again. Check it.

2. Look at the inventory you took at the beginning of your training.

3. Compare the two scores to see how much information you have gained since the beginning of the training.

4. Make a list of areas that you till need to strengthen and plan how this might be done.

Peer Listening Inventory

T F   1. All problems should be discussed with an adult

T F   2. Most problems are very serious.

T F   3. Building trust is an important part of Peer Listening.

T F   4. Put downs are a form of compliment.

T F   5. Every person is important.

T F   6. Every person is unique.

T F   7. All human beings have needs.

T F   8. Capable means able to do.

T F   9. Listening is done only with your ears.

T F 10. You can communicate anger with your eyes.

T F 11. Saying "You must be happy" to an excited person is clarifying that person's feelings.

T F 12. Recognizing your own feelings has nothing to do with the feelings of others.

T F 13. There is one best way to respond to a person with a problem.

T F 14. A good way to respond to someone is to check for feelings.

T F 15. Peer Listeners should put another person's problems ahead of everything in their own lives.

T F 16. You should keep all problems confidential.

T F 17. Consequences are positive and negative outcomes.

T F 18. A Peer Listener should choose an alternative for a friend.

T F 19. Making a decision is easy.

T F 20. When you finish this book, you will need no follow-up training.

Activity 66

Practice Practice

Purpose:

To practice the skills that you learned in this chapter outside the classroom.

Materials:

None

Procedure:

1. Find someone in your school who needs a listener.

2. Using all of the skills you have learned, listen to this person.

3. When you return to your Peer Listening Class, discuss the following questions.

   a. What did the person share with you? (Do not use real names.)

   b. What verbal and non-verbal listening skills did you use?

   c. How did you respond to the person?

   d. Were you able to take care of yourself while listening?

   e. Did you work through the decision-making model?

   f. Did you run into any difficulties? What were they?

Activity 67
Looking at My Skills

Purpose:

> To summarize and evaluate the skills that you learned in this book.

Materials:

> None

Procedure:

1. On this page, write how you feel about your level of skill as a Peer Listener.

2. Write what being a Peer Listener means to you.

3. Write three things that you will take away with you from this training.

4. Write how you plan to use your new skills.

My Reflections:

_____

_____

_____

_____

_____

_____

_____

_____

Activity 68
Closing Ceremony

Purpose:

To recognize accomplishment and evaluate the Peer Listening Experience.

Materials:

None

Purpose:

1. With your class, plan a special celebration of the completion of your Peer Listening Training.

2. Include some of the following suggestions in your plan.

   a. Invite your principal, superintendent, parents, guidance counselor, and others with whom you wish to share your accomplishments.

   b. Ask for volunteers to supply refreshments.

   c. Ask your leader or principal to award certificates of achievement.

   d. Ask for volunteers to read their thoughts from Activity 66 aloud to the class and guests.

   e. Award pins or T shirts to Peer Listeners, if they are available.

Certificate

Name_____

has successfully completed
Peer Listening in the Middle School.

_____ is now recognized
as a Peer Listener by students and faculty at
_____ School.

Signed _____
Date _____

Activity 69

Off We Go

Purpose:

To put closure on your Peer Listening Class.

Materials:

None

Procedure:

1. With your class, stand in a circle and hold hands.

2. Starting with your leader, go around the circle calling out your first name good and loud.

3. When everyone has called out his or her name, say together, "We are Peer Listeners." Still holding hands, raise them up in the air and say together, "Here we go!" "Watch us grow!"

4. Do it again together, loud and strong.

5. Applaud each other.

Notes to Leaders
and Parents

Peer program leaders working with middle school students face a unique challenge. One only has to visit a seventh grade class to understand the dynamic range of physical, cognitive, and emotional development that are dealt with on a daily basis. Our greatest challenges, however, reap the greatest rewards. Nowhere can peer programming have a greater impact than on the diverse population of struggling and emerging youth found in middle schools.

Peer programming is most effectively viewed as a process. Just as students learn progressively more complex concepts around math or language, so can they learn more complex "helping" skills as they move through the educational system.

It is important to define the word "helping," so commonly used to identify peer programs, in terms that are developmentally appropriate to each grade level.

We have, for example, eliminated the term "counseling" from student peer programs at any grade level because it suggests a kind of interaction that requires training and skills not available or appropriate to any of those students. The word "helping" also implies a degree of responsibility in interpersonal relationships that often surpasses the capabilities of the middle school child and is more suitably applied to the high school level. Thus, we have chosen to use the term "Peer Listeners" to apply to participants in peer programs in the middle school.

Research tells us that these eleven, twelve, thirteen, and fourteen year olds want to get involved. Studies also indicate that involvement in meaningful activity reduces the rise of anti-social and self-destructive behavior. One such study identified twelve factors that put children at greatest risk for substance abuse. From these risk factors, they organized a model which denotes bonding as the catalyst for reducing the risk of substance abusing behavior in adolescents. This research suggests that bonding is accomplished through involvement and they further define involvement as an opportunity to serve!

Surveys around substance abuse by adolescents have told us that children who begin using prior to age fifteen are at twice the risk for becoming abusers. Educators know what the research reveals, that middle school students are vulnerable. They are just stepping into the larger world and in doing so they are beginning to make choices that may affect them for the rest of their lives.

It is the degree of capability these students feel in dealing with their everyday world that determines the kind of major, life impacting choices they will ultimately make. Foremost concerns of middle school students are friends, family, and school. If they are connecting with their peers, have a sense of belonging to a group, are successful in some aspects of their school experience, and receive support from their families, they are unlikely to feel the degree of anxiety or despair that leads to choices that are injurious to their futures. Peer programs address many of these concerns both for the Peer Listeners and the students they serve.

We have already noted that "counseling" or "helping" in any constructive sense is not appropriate to either the limited experience or the level of maturity of the middle school student. The exciting news is that these children can be offered opportunities for appropriate service and at the same time practice skills that will serve them in all areas of their lives.

The concept from which peer programs originate goes as far back as the one room school house. In those pioneer days, older children were expected to befriend, listen to, and help their younger and less experienced peers. The primary difference between then and now is systematic training. The need for these kinds of "relationships that serve" are as necessary as ever, but opportunities for these relationships to occur are no longer spontaneous. Peer programs must now be structured in ways that effectively train students for service and effectively monitor the process.

Sandra Peyser Hazouri and Miriam Frey Smith

Specifically, the peer program in the school should have as its goal appropriate opportunities as were referenced in the beginning of this book for students to serve their peers. It must utilize training methods and materials that not only fit the developmental schema but allow for the on-going practice of new skills in the safety of the training setting. Schedules should allow, not only for on-going training, but for follow-up and monitoring of the activities that are the end result of the training. These criteria are the basis for the development of *Peer Listening in the Middle School*

The focus of the activities in *Peer Listening in the Middle School* is on the everyday problems of the middle school student. Most concerns of these students are centered around friends, school, and family. They are issues of adjustment, competency, and acceptability.

"Am I wearing the right clothes?"

"What if my parents won't let me go?"

"Does he like me?"

"I don't understand math!"

Indeed, a recent Missouri study (Sportsman 1987) found the foremost worry of sixth graders about to enter middle school had to do with using a locker for the first time.

From an adult perspective, these issues may seem trivial. However it is important to remember that these concerns are developmentally inspired and as such are very significant to the maturing process of the young adolescent. A good listener can effectively reduce the anxiety and stress around these issues.

There are more critical concerns that middle school students deal with as well. Change, relationships, and decisions can be disturbing and disruptive to this inexperienced population of young people.

"My best friend is moving."

"Should I drink beer?"

"I am in love with him."

These are the issues that most prevention programs target. They have the potential to become major problems for adolescents. Emotional trauma can lead to depression; substance use can lead to abuse; and early sexual activity may result in promiscuity or pregnancy. Training will provide Peer Listeners with the skill needed to identify those problems requiring adult intervention.

There are, of course, some sad and serious problems among our middle school population. They are most often family problems of dysfunction. The children who are the victims of the dysfunction suffer from all forms of abuse and neglect. These problems are not within the realm of the Peer Listener. However, they may be encountered along with the myriad everyday problems of middle school. Consistent monitoring by the adults involved in the program will insure appropriate handling of these problems. Training will prepare students to refer these serious issues to adults and to share any questions raised during listening encounters.

Peer Listening in the Middle School is designed to fit a nine-week elective course. It is equally appropriate, however, to after school programs, advisement programs, and youth groups. Many of the activities in this book can be correlated in the curriculum areas of language arts, social studies, and health. The activities offer a myriad of opportunities for cooperative and experiential learning and for physical movement.

The success of a Peer Listening Group many be determined in a number of ways: the ongoing and visible support of school administrators and staff; the ability of the group to regenerate after its first year in existence; the number of students who identify with or want to become Peer Listeners; and how well Peer Listeners reflects the social, ethnic, and gender balance of the school population. The presence of one or more of these factors suggests that a peer program is experiencing some degree of success. All of these factors are impacted by the leader's or sponsor's efforts in marketing the peer program and monitoring its efforts.

The authors of *Peer Listening in the Middle School* wish you and your children success with your program.

Bibliography

1. Foster, E.S. (1989). *Energizers and ice breakers.* Minneapolis, MN: Educational Media Corporation.

2. Freeman, S.M. (1989). *From peer pressure to peer support.* Minneapolis, MN: Johnson Institute Books.

3. Hawkins, J.D., Lishner, D.M., Catalano, R.F., and Howard, M.O. (1985). Childhood predictors of adolescent substance abuse: Toward empirically grounded theory. *Journal of Contemporary Society.*

4. Myrick, R.D. and Erney, T. (1978, 1984). *Caring and sharing: Becoming a peer facilitator.* Minneapolis, MN: Educational Media Corporation.

5. Myrick, R.D. and Bowman, R.P., (1981). *Becoming a friendly helper: A handbook for student facilitators.* Minneapolis, MN: Educational Media Corporation.

6. Myrick, R.D. and Folk, B.E. (1991). *Peervention: Training peer facilitators for prevention education.* Minneapolis, MN: Educational Media Corporation.

7. Sportsman, S.J. (1987). What worries kids about the next level. *Middle School Journal, 18*:34-5.

8. Stone, J.D. and Keefauver, L. (1990). *Friend to friend: Helping your friends through problems.* Minneapolis, MN: Educational Media Corporation.

9. Williams, Margery. (1985) *The velveteen rabbit.* New York, NY: Random House, Inc.

Sandra Peyser Hazouri and Miriam Frey Smith